Play Foundations

Journeys

Gray

Acknowledgements

© 2008 Folens Limited, on behalf of the author.

United Kingdom: Folens Publishers, Waterslade House, Thame Road, Haddenham, Buckinghamshire HP17 8NT.

Email: folens@folens.com

Ireland: Folens Publishers, Greenhills Road, Tallaght, Dublin 24.

Email: info@folens.ie

Commissioning editor: Zoë Nichols
Managing editor: Jane Morgan   Editor: Jane Bishop
Design and layout: Infuze Ltd   Illustrations: Gaynor Berry
Cover design: Infuze Ltd   Cover illustration: Cathy Hughes

With thanks to the following for their permission to use extracts:

All Early learning goals and Aspects of learning quoted in this book are taken from *Practice Guidance for the Early Years Foundation Stage* (Department for Education and Skills) and are reproduced under the terms of the Click-Use Licence.

First published 2008 by Folens Limited.

British Library Cataloguing in Publication Data. A catalogue record for this publication is available from the British Library.

ISBN 978-1-85008-333-7

Contents

Introduction   4
Planning chart   6
Assessment ideas   8
Observation hints   9

Chapter 1: Transport
The driving seat   10
Car game ✎   11
Times and signs   12
Tickets ✎   13
Land, sea or air?   14
Ready, steady, go!   15
Where am I going?   16
Making tracks   17

Chapter 2: Out and about
Going to the doctor's   18
My journey   19
Taking the train   20
Out of the window ✎   21
Going to the shops   22
Sort the shopping ✎   23
Malleable maps   24
The ticket office   25

Chapter 3: Going on holiday
Ready to go   26
All aboard!   27
The passport trail   28
Passport ✎   29
Are we nearly there?   30
Countryside scene ✎   31
It's a long way   32
Seaside picture   33

Chapter 4: Animal journeys
Finding food   34
The swallow's journey   35
From pond to bush   36
Frogs in the pond ✎   37
Penguin partners   38
Whales and dolphins   39
Horse and cart   40
Working horses ✎   41

Chapter 5: Storybook journeys
Little Red Riding Hood   42
Doing the rounds   43
Off to the shops   44
Going to nursery ✎   45
Gruffalo maps   46
Under, over and through   47
Under the sea   48

Introduction

Who the book is for

This book forms part of the *Play Foundations* series which provides guidance for practitioners to set up quality play scenarios or activities with young children. It is written for all those working with three-, four- and five-year-old children in a variety of settings. Although many of the activities are written with nursery or school settings in mind, they can easily be adapted for childminders working with children in their homes. The book will be of particular interest to all those working within the Early Years Foundation Stage (EYFS) framework. It will also be useful for parents*.

Learning through play

The activities in this book are based on the EYFS principles:

- Each child is unique and is a competent learner from birth.
- Positive relationships ensure that children learn to be strong and independent.
- Enabling environments play a key role in extending learning and development.
- Learning and development takes many different forms and all areas are connected.

The focus of the activities is on child-initiated learning and the emphasis is on process rather than product. There are suggestions for using your guidance, your language and your support to promote the children's learning as they explore and play. Many of the activities can be enjoyed outside. Being outside has a positive impact on children's sense of well-being and can help all aspects of development.

How to use this book

The book is divided into five chapters, each focusing on a different aspect of the theme of journeys, with each chapter providing a range of activities that support all areas of children's learning and development.

The chapters are:

- Transport
- Out and about
- Going on holiday
- Animal journeys
- Storybook journeys.

The activities

Each chapter has six activities, each focusing on one or two Areas of learning and development. The activities give a specific Early learning goal for each learning focus. Most of the activities are designed for small groups of around four children, often with introductions that are suitable for the whole group to take part in. In cases where individuals require more support, or when using limited equipment (such as computers) it may be relevant to work with just one or two children.

Each activity is divided into the following sections:

- To help to plan *Enabling environments*, there is a section on *Setting up*, outlining the resources needed and how to set up.
- *Getting started* describes how to organise the actual activity.

- *Let's talk!* provides ideas for talking with the children about their experiences including questions that could be asked and how to differentiate language to suit the children's varying abilities. There are also suggestions for making the most of assessment opportunities.
- Recognising *A unique child* and *Positive relationships* means making sure that self-esteem, confidence and relationships remain positive and there are *Top tips* for doing so.
- The *Differentiation* section includes ideas for personalising the learning by adjusting each activity to make it easier for those children needing support or more challenging for others. This section will also be useful for planning inclusive activities for those children who have special or additional needs.
- *Further ideas* for each activity suggest ways of extending and enhancing learning and development opportunities.
- Photocopiable activity sheets are provided in the book and they can also be printed from the CD-ROM. They are intended to enhance children's play or to create game scenarios.
- Every activity page includes a Claude Cat box, which lists relevant resources on the CD-ROM.

The importance of ICT

Nowadays, young children are becoming increasingly familiar with using ICT as part of their everyday experiences. Stories, rhymes and songs can be enjoyed through television and computer programs, and many early years settings have interactive whiteboard facilities. Children are surrounded by texts that combine images, sounds and words both on screen and paper and they need to learn to read images as well as print. The CD-ROM that accompanies this book provides opportunities for children to explore and become familiar with visual text, photographic and drawn still images, moving images, sound and colour.

Using the CD-ROM

The CD-ROM has been designed for children to use with adult support.

Claude Cat

Claude Cat gives instructions or asks questions which are designed to encourage children to verbalise their observations, ideas and understanding. This will help you to assess whether they need further support or challenge.

The main menu

This screen has the option to select a theme.

The theme menu

When the theme screen is displayed, you have the option of selecting different resources, for example, an interactive picture, story, rhyme or song, by clicking on the appropriate icon:

 Songs   Rhymes   Stories   Activity sheets   Interactive pictures   Photos (some have sound)   Film clips

* Whenever the term 'parent' is used this is taken to include parents and/or the children's primary carers.

Planning chart

Use this chart to help with your planning. Each activity focuses on one or two Area(s) of learning and development. These are highlighted by the stars shown on the chart. The Areas of learning and development are divided up into 'aspects' and the aspect(s) for each activity are also provided on the chart. On the activity pages you will also find an 'Early learning goal' objective for each activity.

The following key is used on the activity pages:

 PSED: Personal, social and emotional development

 KUW: Knowledge and understanding of the world

 CLL: Communication, language and literacy

 PD: Physical development

 PSRN: Problem solving, reasoning and numeracy

 CD: Creative development

Activities	Areas of learning and development							Aspect of learning
Transport	Page	PSED	CLL	PSRN	KUW	PD	CD	**Aspect of learning**
The driving seat	10	★						Making relationships
Times and signs	12		★					Writing
							★	Developing imagination and imaginative play
Land, sea or air?	14			★				Shape, space and measures
Ready, steady, go!	15				★			Exploration and investigation
			★					Language for thinking
Where am I going?	16					★		Movement and space
Making tracks	17						★	Exploring media and materials
				★				Shape, space and measures
Out and about	Page	PSED	CLL	PSRN	KUW	PD	CD	**Aspect of learning**
Going to the doctor's	18	★						Self-confidence and self-esteem
My journey	19				★			Place
				★				Shape, space and measures
Taking the train	20		★					Linking sounds and letters
Going to the shops	22			★				Numbers as labels and for counting
			★					Language for communication
Malleable maps	24					★		Using equipment and materials
The ticket office	25						★	Developing imagination and imaginative play
						★		Movement and space

Going on holiday	Page	PSED	CLL	PSRN	KUW	PD	CD	Aspect of learning
Ready to go	26	★						Self-care
All aboard!	27				★			Designing and making
						★		Using equipment and materials
The passport trail	28		★					Writing
Are we nearly there?	30			★				Shape, space and measures
It's a long way	32					★		Movement and space
							★	Developing imagination and imaginative play
Seaside picture	33						★	Developing imagination and imaginative play
					★			Place

Animal journeys	Page	PSED	CLL	PSRN	KUW	PD	CD	Aspect of learning
Finding food	34	★						Self-confidence and self-esteem
					★			Exploration and investigation
The swallow's journey	35		★					Reading
					★			Place
From pond to bush	36			★				Calculating
Penguin partners	38				★			Exploration and investigation
Whales and dolphins	39						★	Creating music and dance
Horse and cart	40					★		Using equipment and materials
				★				Time

Storybook journeys	Page	PSED	CLL	PSRN	KUW	PD	CD	Aspect of learning
Little Red Riding Hood	42	★						Self-care
			★					Language for communication
Doing the rounds	43			★				Shape, space and measures
Off to the shops	44		★					Reading
Gruffalo maps	46				★			Place
							★	Exploring media and materials
Under, over and through	47					★		Movement and space
		★						Making relationships
Under the sea	48						★	Being creative – responding to experiences and expressing and communicating ideas

Assessment ideas

Young children are individuals first, each with a unique profile of abilities. All the planning that we do should flow from the observations that we make on an ongoing basis and these will help us to understand and consider their current interests, development and learning.

How to assess children

Observing children during their daily routines allows us to note their responses in different situations and to different people. In some settings, a specific Area of learning and development is targeted and the key person is asked to observe what stage the children in their care have reached over the next day or week, revisiting that Area from time to time. Others use sticky notes in order to capture relevant observations. These can be collated later by a key person and entered into the ongoing records for the child. Others still make use of photography, daily diaries, activity feedback sheets or tracking records to capture the children's progress at different times. There is no prescribed method and you will find methods that suit your practice and the children and families concerned.

Planning for assessment

Through assessment you can see what stages the children have reached in their learning and development and therefore work out the best resources, opportunities and activities to plan next. Sometimes this might involve planning a specific activity to enable the child to take their learning that little bit further, or it may be necessary to plan a similar activity in order to reinforce learning further, before moving on. Sometimes it will simply mean providing the right opportunities and observing the children as they play and learn independently. You will find a mixture of adult-led and child-led activities in the activity chapters with suggestions for you to observe and assess the children within the *Let's talk!* sections of each page.

Using your assessments

Once you have observed the children at play, analyse your observations and highlight the children's achievements or their need for further support. Assessments are the decisions you make using what you have observed about each child's development and learning. You are asked to involve parents as part of the ongoing observation and assessment process and it is also helpful to share your plans for the short-term (a week) and long-term (a term) planning. Your planning should always follow the same pattern – observe, analyse and reflect, then use what you have found out to plan next steps in the child's learning. In this way you can personalise the children's learning and make the most of their strengths, interests and needs.

The 'Look, listen and note' approach of the EYFS is a helpful tool when deciding what to observe and how. On the next page, this format has been applied to children learning about 'journeys' so that you can begin to think about how your assessment and observations of children within this theme can feed back into your planning. For each of the five chapter headings there are ideas for what you should look out for especially.

Observation hints

Here are some suggestions to help you focus your observations and assessments when learning about 'journeys'.

Chapter heading	Look, listen and note
Transport	• Observe whether children are able to play independently or whether they look to an adult or others for support. • Listen to the vocabulary that the children use to describe how they have sorted their vehicles. Can they explain their criteria? • Make a note of children's ability to move imaginatively as vehicles. Do they make good use of the space available?
Out and about	• Observe whether the children use number words in their play. Do they count and solve simple mathematical problems in imaginative play? • Listen to the way the children talk about a remembered experience. Are they able to express their feelings? • Make a note of children's ability to segment a word and hear individual phonemes. Can they write any simple CVC words?
Going on holiday	• Observe whether the children are able to select the materials they need for making a model vehicle. Are they capable of fixing the materials together? • Listen to the children's explanations for their choice of clothes. Are they able to link one thing to another to explain their ideas? • Make a note of children's ability to apply one-to-one correspondence between the number of passengers and the objects they require. Note how many objects they are able to count in an irregular arrangement.
Animal journeys	• Observe whether the children are confident in using a range of equipment. Do they find new and imaginative ways to use objects? • Listen to the children as they report the information that they have found out about penguins. Look for evidence of a growing vocabulary and awareness of the listener as they speak. • Make a note of whether the children are able to apply their mathematical understanding in practical contexts.
Storybook journeys	• Observe if the children are able to play independently, making choices about games to play and how to set up a themed role-play area. • Listen to how the children describe shapes. Do they use describing words? Do they know the names of the shapes? Are they able to apply a chosen criteria to sort objects? • Make a note of whether the children understand the terms 'beginning' and 'end'. Are they able to retell the main points of a simple story?

Transport The driving seat

CD-ROM resources

 Car game

Busy town

Early learning goal

Work as part of a group or class, taking turns and sharing fairly, understanding that there needs to be agreed values and codes of behaviour for groups of people, including adults and children, to work together harmoniously.

Setting up

On to the surface of your outdoor area, chalk a road big enough for the large wheeled toys to drive inside. Provide two or three large wheeled toys. Put out a box of dressing-up clothes suitable for 'going on an outing'. Set up a 'destination' such as a play shop.

Getting started

- Before the children go outside, take turns to talk about outings that they have been on. Work with a small group of children at a time and show them the road that you have drawn. Explain that they can take turns to use the road to go on an outing to the shop.
- Show them the dressing-up box and tell them that they may dress up, or choose a bag or a hat, before they go. Explain that one or two of the children may play in the shop while they wait for their turn.
- Leave the children to talk about what they will do, negotiating roles and deciding who will go first. Allow the children to play freely, making sure that all the children have the opportunity to join in. If necessary, remind the children of some simple rules for playing together cooperatively.

Let's talk!

Say, *Tell me about an outing you have been on.* For children requiring more support, ask *Will there be enough room for everyone to go at once?* For children requiring challenge, ask *What different things are there to do? How can we share out the jobs?* Notice how individual children join in with the activity. Do the children understand why they need to take turns? Note which children are able to play without your support and those who look to you for confirmation of their ideas.

Top tip

Understand that some children may find it difficult to guide the vehicle within the lines and suggest that they make their own journey to the shop. Model how to accept the various ideas that the children have for their play.

Differentiation

Provide support for children by suggesting roles and establishing who will go first and so on. Provide an extra challenge by inviting the children to use chalks to add further roads or buildings.

Further ideas

- Show individuals how to play with the interactive picture, 'Busy town', on the CD-ROM.
- Play the game on photocopiable page 11 and help the children to take turns to throw the dice and move small cars or counters into the garage. If they land on the crossing they miss a turn.

Car game

Throw the dice to move
your car to the garage.

Garage

start

Times and signs

CD-ROM resources

Tickets

Road signs

Setting up

With the children's help, set up your role-play area as a ticket office (include timetables, leaflets and tickets) and make copies of the activity sheet on page 13 or print them from the CD-ROM. Provide large chalks in your outside area and make giant signposts (such as 'stop' and 'go' signs) from bamboo canes and card circles. Fill a dressing-up box with police officer/traffic warden outfits. Provide clipboards, paper and pens in a box.

Getting started

- Show the children the photo of the road signs. Find out what they know and understand about signs in the environment. Talk about the ticket and sign templates and the materials in the role-play area and ask the children for ideas of how they will play with them. Explain that there are chalks for drawing roads and signs and dressing-up clothes and clipboards for them to use. Ask an adult to go into role with the children to enhance their play and encourage play writing.
- Go outside with a group of children and join in their play, showing them the signposts you have made and letting them use these and other resources in their imaginative play.
- Encourage mark-making on the outside surface and model how to use the clipboards to write down registration numbers, make bookings and record good driving!

Let's talk!

Ask, *What do we need road signs for?* For children requiring more support, ask *Can you get me some tickets from the ticket office?* Challenge the children by asking, *Can you make me a ticket to travel to the zoo today?* Notice how individual children write in their play. Do they attempt to write words, making use of their phonic knowledge? Do they use drawings to communicate meaning? Do they use writing for a variety of purposes?

Top tip

Use the opportunity to talk to the children about keeping safe near roads. Discuss safe places to cross and how they must never cross roads without an adult. Together decide on some safety rules for using the wheeled toys in your setting.

Differentiation

Support children by drawing their attention to the signs and writing that you can see around the setting. Talk about what they represent. Set further challenges such as making holiday posters and brochures and creating giant signposts with writing.

Further ideas

- Make miniature signs for use with road mats and small world play.
- Make and use signs to signify regular activities at your setting, such as an apple and cup picture for snack time; a piano for singing time.

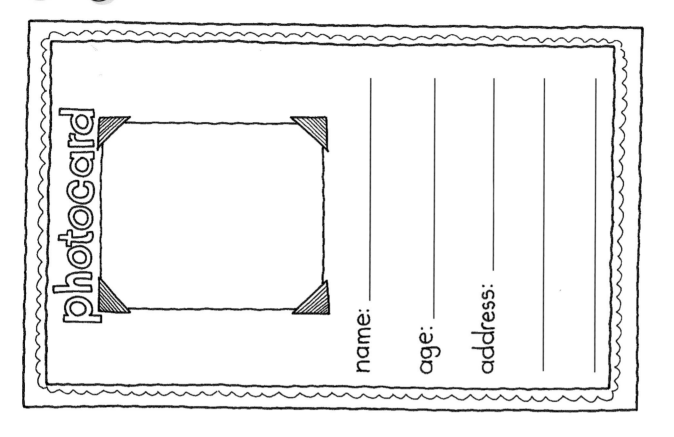

photocard

name: _____

age: _____

address: _____
_____

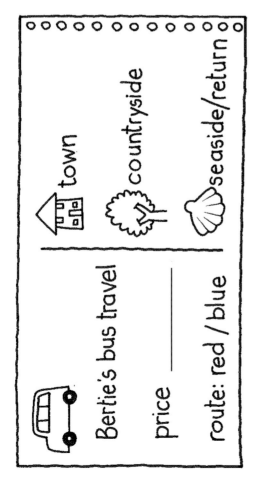

Bertie's bus travel

town

countryside

seaside/return

price _____

route: red / blue

price _____

date _____

Admit one child to GRAY'S ZOO

Land, sea or air?

CD-ROM resources

♪ Down at the station

Early learning goal

Use developing mathematical ideas and methods to solve practical problems.

Setting up
Make a collection of vehicles (boats, cars, lorries, vans, trains, aeroplanes and so on) and place them in a large box on a carpeted area. Provide a range of sorting trays or containers next to the box.

Getting started
- Listen to the song 'Down at the station' on the CD-ROM, talk about the vehicles in the song and make up some actions.
- Allow small groups of children at a time to play freely with the vehicles in the box. Talk to individual children or pairs about the vehicles. Ask the children to name them and tell you if they go on land, in the sea or in the air. Examine some of the vehicles to decide what helps them to move (wings, wheels and so on).
- Now ask the children to make a small collection of vehicles and put them in a tray. Tell them that the vehicles all need to belong together for some reason (it could be colour, size, type of vehicle or anything else that the children choose). Ask the children to tell you and each other about their collections. Allow the children to play freely with the vehicles again.

Let's talk!
Say, *Tell me about your favourite kind of car. What do you know about trains? Can you guess why Georgia has put those vehicles in a group?* For children requiring more support, ask *Can you find me a vehicle with wheels? Can you find me another one?* For children requiring challenge, ask *Can you sort all the vehicles into three groups? Is there more than one way to do this?* Notice the vocabulary that the children use when describing how they have arranged their vehicles. Are they able to make a range of connections between the various vehicles?

Top tip
Demonstrate how you listen carefully to each child's ideas and show respect for what they have to say. For example, *That's interesting Joshua; you have chosen all red vehicles. Well done!* Encourage the children to listen to each other's ideas without interrupting them. Be aware that some children may prefer to line up groups of objects rather than placing them in piles.

Differentiation
Provide support by specifying the sorting criteria for the child. For example, ask her to make a collection of cars or a group of red vehicles. Provide an extra challenge by making a collection yourself and asking the children to explain why you have made that group.

Further ideas
- Provide building blocks and invite the children to make buildings such as garages, stations, airports or harbours. Suggest that they match the vehicles to the buildings.

Ready, steady, go!

CD-ROM resources

The wheels on the bus

Early learning goals

Ask questions about why things happen and how things work.

Use talk to organise, sequence and clarify thinking, ideas, feelings and events.

Setting up

Set up an interest table of 'things that go' and let the children use them for free play. Include some plastic vehicles that can be dismantled easily as well as some vehicles made from materials such as LEGO. Collect a box of reclaimed and craft materials suitable for making model vehicles, as well as glue, scissors and sticky tape.

Getting started

- Gather the children around your display table and invite individuals to choose a vehicle. Can they demonstrate how it goes? What can they tell everyone about it? Sing the song 'The wheels on the bus' (on the CD-ROM) together and talk about other vehicles that need wheels to move.
- In small groups, invite the children to help you dismantle some of the vehicles, talking together about how they move. Now let them experiment with the reclaimed materials and craft equipment. Ask them to try and make something that goes, such as a car, a bus, a boat or a plane.
- Be on hand to help the children with their designs. Give them the freedom to experiment with fixing the materials together, but offer help and suggestions when necessary in order to enhance their play.

Let's talk!

Say, *Tell me about the vehicles on the table. How do they move?* For children requiring more support, ask *Show me how to make this toy vehicle move. How did you do that?* For children requiring an extra challenge ask *What materials is this vehicle made from? What materials are used to make other kinds of vehicles?* Notice if the children are able to describe the movement of the vehicles. Are they curious to find out more? Do they understand the relationship of cause and effect when describing how to make the toys move or work?

Top tip

Look out for children who have a passion for toy cars and vehicles. Listen to their comments and encourage them to tell you more about their interest. Notice which children are particularly interested in vehicles and pair them together to play freely with the vehicles in order to develop a new friendship.

Differentiation

Help children who require more support to sort a selection of objects into things that go and things that do not move. Provide an extra challenge by inviting the children to follow some instructions to build a model of something that moves, such as a Duplo vehicle.

Further ideas

- Play a traffic light movement game outside, with the children pretending to be vehicles as you call out the colours *red* (stop), *amber* (change directions) and *green* (go)!

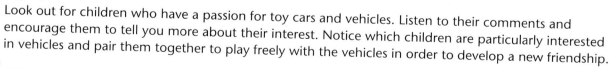

Where am I going?

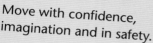
Early learning goal
Move with confidence, imagination and in safety.

Setting up
Arrange to work in a large, safe and empty space, indoors or outdoors.

Getting started

- Ask the children to sit where they can see your computer or whiteboard screen clearly and play the film clip. Invite the children to comment on what they have just watched. Ask the children to tell you about any types of transport they have travelled on.
- Invite volunteers to tell the rest of the group about a journey they have made. Encourage them to describe the mode of transport and what the journey was like and where they were going.
- Now go to your large clear space and encourage the children to spread out. Explain to them that you are going to ask them to move like different vehicles. For example, a bus stopping and starting as it picks up and drops off passengers, a tractor chugging along slowly and a racing car speeding along, dodging obstacles and other cars!
- Stop the children from time to time and ask children who have been moving with care and imagination to show their movements to the rest of the group.
- Play some 'jolly' music and allow the children to move freely, pretending to be any vehicle they wish.

Let's talk!
Say, *Tell me about a really fast/slow journey you have made. How might it feel to fly in an aeroplane?* For children requiring more support, ask *How did you travel to the group today? Can you show me what the journey was like?* Challenge the children by asking, *Tell me about three different types of transport you have been in.* Notice how the children use the space. Are they able to spread out and use the space safely? Look for individual ideas and imaginative use of the space.

Top tip
Be aware that some children may have had limited first-hand experience of different kinds of transport. Draw on their knowledge of what they have seen in the street or in television programmes. Let parents know that you will be discussing transport and encourage them to talk with their children about journeys they have made.

Differentiation
Provide support for children who find it hard to move imaginatively by demonstrating some of your ideas first, and allowing them to copy your movements. Provide an extra challenge by inviting the children to make up a sequence of movements for their favourite form of transport.

Further ideas
- Make a list together of all the types of transport that you can spot in the 'busy city' film clip.
- Show pictures of different vehicles, play music and ask the children to move like the vehicle that you are showing them.

Making tracks

Setting up

Set up your painting area with dishes of brightly-coloured paint, aprons, pieces of paper in different sizes, sponge transport shapes, small world vehicles, pieces of LEGO and small wheels. Make your own print using some of the objects.

Getting started

- Talk about the photo on the CD-ROM. What materials can the children see? What is the child doing? How are the materials being used?
- Show the children the print you have made. Can they guess how you achieved that effect? What objects do they think you used?
- Work with small groups at a time and encourage them to experiment with the different objects. Show them how to dip the wheels in paint and roll them along the paper.
- Allow the children to experiment and work freely, taking care not to mix up the paint colours.

Let's talk!

Talk together about the colours and paint effects that the children are making. For children requiring more support, ask *What colours have you used?* For children requiring challenge, say *Describe the shapes you have made on your paper. Do you have mostly straight or curvy shapes?* Notice how much the children experiment, do they explore the objects and use them in more than one way? Can they describe what they are doing and have they planned their designs? Do they know the names of the colours?

Top tip

Understand that some children will not like getting their hands messy. Provide a damp cloth or paper towels for them to wipe their fingers on at intervals and show them how aprons will keep their clothes clean. Conversely, other children will need reminding to take care with the equipment, to be mindful of other children in not mixing up the colours and to wash their hands clean afterwards.

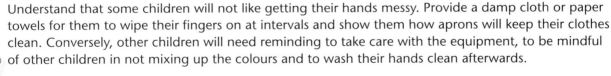

Differentiation

Be on hand to help children who need support by showing them how to apply just enough paint to make a print without the paint smudging and running. Help them to take care not to mix up the colours by keeping the objects next to the paint they have been dipped into. Use the opportunity to practise recognising colours. Provide an extra challenge by inviting the children to use the equipment to make a picture or a repeating pattern with the printing objects.

Further ideas

- Print repeating patterns of transport shapes on long strips of paper. Use the borders to add interest to a wall frieze or display.
- Make a book of patterns together, sticking in interesting pieces of fabric, wallpaper and patterned paper.

CD-ROM resources

Ambulance

Here comes the helicopter

Early learning goal

Respond to significant experiences, showing a range of feelings when appropriate.

Setting up

With the children's help, set up your role-play area as a doctor's surgery. In your outdoor area put out large wheeled vehicles and add signs or stickers to some of them to create 'emergency vehicles'.

Getting started

- Talk about 'people who help us', such as fire fighters, health visitors and so on. Talk about the journeys that these people make – some have to go very fast, using sirens to warn people and some need special vehicles. Show the children the photo of the ambulance and listen to the sound. Talk about it together.
- Next listen to the rhyme 'Here comes the helicopter' on the CD-ROM, say it together and help the children to learn it. Now ask the children to take turns to tell you about a visit to the doctor's. Encourage them to use a range of vocabulary to express how they felt.
- Allow the children to take turns to play freely in the doctor's role-play area to act out scenarios of going to the doctor's; and also in the outside area to pretend to be ambulance drivers, fire fighters and so on.

Let's talk!

Say, *Tell me about an emergency that you have seen or know about. Why might an ambulance need to go fast and use its siren?* For children requiring more support, ask *Tell me about a time when you felt poorly. Who helped you?* Challenge the children to solve some problems such as, *You have just seen a young boy fall off his bicycle and bump his head. What should you do next? Who do you need to call? What would you tell them?* Notice if the children are able to express their feelings about a remembered experience. Tune in to the way the children express their concerns and worries.

Top tip

Some children may find it hard to talk about their past experiences, but will find it easier to role-play a remembered situation. Encourage the children to show care and concern for their friends.

Differentiation

Provide support by going into role with the children and asking them simple questions to support the imaginative play. Provide an extra challenge by inviting the children to perform their role-play scenario in front of the group.

Further ideas

- Print out the photo from the CD-ROM and make a display of people who help us. Add small world emergency vehicles and a selection of non-fiction and fiction books such as *Topsy and Tim Go to the Doctor* by Jean Adamson and Gareth Adamson (Ladybird).

My journey

CD-ROM resources

Family in the park

Early learning goals

Observe, find out about and identify features in the place they live and the natural world.

Use everyday words to describe position.

Setting up

Set up an interest table with different kinds of maps. Add photos that show the children travelling to the group (ask parents to provide these). Set out some road and town layout mats with small world vehicles, play people and small world buildings if available.

Getting started

- Ask the children to tell a partner about their journey to the group and invite some children to tell their journey to the whole group. Find out about the things that the children pass on the way to the group. Encourage them to use positional and geographical vocabulary, such as *past the pond*, *round the corner*, *next to the telephone box* and so on. Look at the photos of the children's

journeys and help the children to identify things that they recognise in the pictures.
- Play the film clip for the children to watch, talk together about the places and objects that the children can see.
- Now ask the children in pairs or small groups to use the road and town mats and small world toys to act out their journey to your setting. Encourage them to talk about their journey as they play.

Let's talk!

Say, *Show me what your journey to the group looks like. How do you get here each day? What things do you pass on the way?* For children requiring more support, ask *Tell me about one thing that you see on your way to the group.* For children requiring an extra challenge, ask *What buildings do you pass on the way to the group? What are they used for?* Notice if the children are able to connect photos to places in the environment. Can they represent (in simple terms) their walk or journey using small world toys and other objects? The emphasis at this stage should be on using relevant vocabulary rather than on accurate mapping skills.

Top tip

Foster the children's sense of belonging in the group by asking them to provide a caption to go with the photo they have brought in from home. Help the children to make connections in their learning by using the small world toys to represent their experiences of travelling to the group.

Differentiation

Support younger children by playing alongside them and using some simple geographical words to describe the journey of the small world toys. Provide an extra challenge by inviting the children to draw a simple map showing a journey they make regularly.

Further ideas

- Help the children to program a Roamer or a floor turtle to move along a simple route.

Taking the train

CD-ROM resources

 Out of the window

 Busy station

Early learning goal

 Use their phonic knowledge to write simple regular words and make phonetically plausible attempts at more complex words.

Setting up

Make a simple book for each child using an A4 piece of sugar paper and a piece of plain paper. Fold the sugar paper to make a book cover. Insert the folded plain paper and staple together. Make a copy of the activity sheet 'Out of the window' on page 21 or print from the CD-ROM for each child.

Getting started

- Show the whole group the photo of the busy station from the CD-ROM. Talk about where the children think it is and what they can see and listen to the sound facility together. Ask the children if they have ever been on a train. Invite them to tell the rest of the group about their experiences.
- Show the children the pictures on the activity sheet 'Out of the window'. Talk about the order that they might go in. Work with small groups at a time to cut out and stick the pictures in the home-made books in their chosen order and let the children explain their story to you.
- Invite them to design a cover for their book and encourage them to write any words or add any letters to the cover and pages to tell the story of the journey. Help them to sound out the words to make reasonable attempts.

Let's talk!

Say, *Tell me what you can see in the photo. Tell me about a train journey you have been on. What might you see from a train window?* For children requiring more support, ask *Tell me three things you can see in the photo.* Challenge the children by asking *Tell me the story that you have made with the pictures.* Are the children able to decide on a sequence for the pictures? Are they able to segment a word and hear individual phonemes? Can they relate the phonemes to letters? Are they able to write the letters? Can they write any simple CVC words?

Top tip

Give the children time to think about the order in which they want to put the pictures, giving them the space to explore all their ideas. Make sure that most of the discussion comes from the children. Allow them to explore their own ideas fully before you intervene with questions.

Differentiation

Support children by helping them to hear the initial phonemes in words. Point to the matching letter on an alphabet chart and show them how to form it correctly. To challenge the children, ask them to write one or two sentences to go with each picture.

Further ideas

- Share the song 'Down at the station' also found on the CD-ROM in the 'Transport' theme.

20

Journeys

Out of the window

Cut out the pictures. Put them in order.

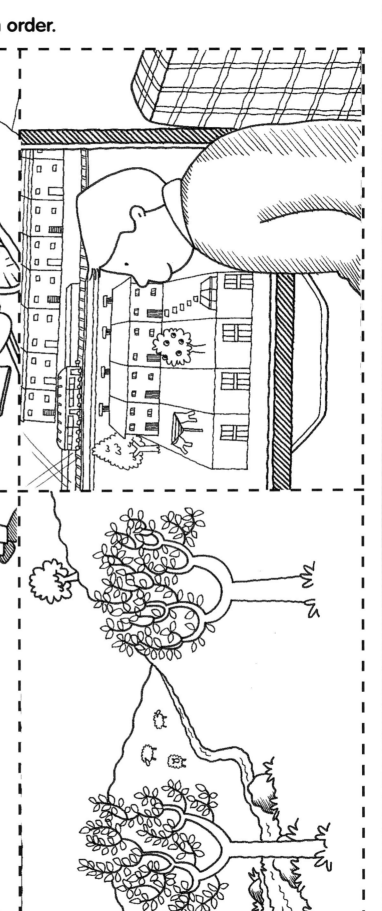

Going to the shops

Early learning goals

Say and use number names in order in familiar contexts.

Enjoy listening to and using spoken and written language, and readily turn to it in their play and learning.

Setting up

With the children's help, set up a shop in your outdoor play area or role-play corner. Stock it with play food and shopping baskets. Make an A3 copy of the activity sheet, 'Sort the shopping' from page 23 or print from the CD-ROM, colour it and laminate it, cutting out the individual cards.

Getting started

- Invite the children to take turns to talk about their experiences of going shopping. Now play a memory game and start the chant: *When I went shopping I put one banana in my basket.* Invite the next child in the circle to repeat the phrase adding an object of their own. Continue until everyone has had a turn, encouraging the children to try to remember the whole list (helpful prompts are allowed!).
- Next show the children the laminated activity sheet. Decide on the game you wish to play with it (put in objects for the children to count; use it to sort the objects into groups; use it for addition or take away sums). Continue the work with small groups at a time, and give them their own sheet and cards to experiment with.
- Allow the children to take turns to use the role-play shop. Encourage them to role-play as customers and shop keepers, adding objects to their baskets, counting them and so on.

Let's talk!

Say, *Tell me about a time when you helped your mum or dad at the shops. How did you get there? Describe the set of objects you have put in your basket.* Support children by asking *Can you find me another one of these? How many do I have now?* Challenge the children to tell you how they have sorted the shopping. Notice if the children use number words in their play. Are they able to count out a specified number of objects from a larger group?

Top tip

Use the opportunity to talk about food that keeps us healthy. Include a range of different ethnic foods in your role-play shop (ask parents to supply packaging of the children's healthy favourites).

Differentiation

Provide support by specifying the sorting criteria for the child. Provide an extra challenge by making a collection yourself and asking the children to explain your choice.

Further ideas

- Make some laminated shopping lists with pictures and numbers (such as an apple with the number 3 beside it). Attach wipe-clean pens to the lists. The children can use them to 'go shopping' in the role-play area, using the wipe-clean pens to make notes, cross or tick off and so on.

Sort the shopping

Choose some things to put in the basket.

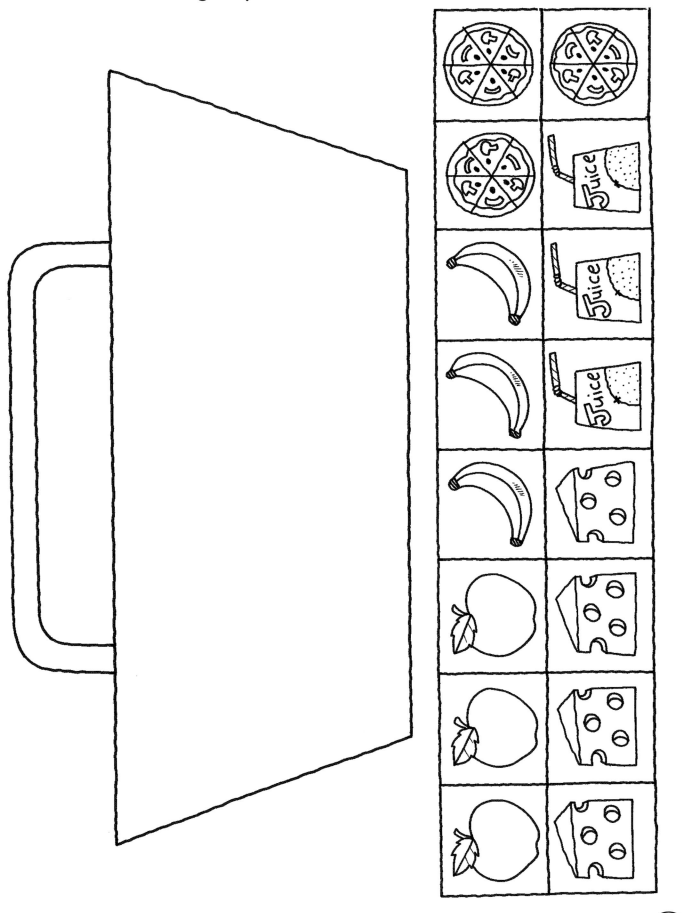

Malleable maps

Early learning goal

Handle tools, objects, construction and malleable materials safely and with increasing control.

Setting up

Draw some simple road layouts on to large pieces of card and laminate them (or use plastic printed road layout mats). Provide play dough in a range of colours.

Getting started

- Ask the children to come and sit where they can see your computer or whiteboard screen clearly. Look at the photo together. Talk about what the girl is looking at and what we use maps for. Think about the sort of information that it is useful to show on a map, such as roads, rivers, woods, big buildings and so on.
- Provide groups of two or three children with road layouts and play dough and explain that you would like them to add some detail to the map, such as woods, ponds, buildings – anything they want!
- Practise rolling, squeezing, pulling, twisting, snipping and scraping the play dough to make objects for the road layout maps. Show the children one or two suggestions of your own to help to get them started.
- As you work alongside the groups, talk to the children about journeys they have made and maps they have seen being used.

Let's talk!

Ask, *What things have you put on your map? Does your map remind you of a place that you have been to?* For children requiring more support, ask *Tell me about one thing you have made.* Challenge the children by asking them, *Can you describe the technique you used to make your tree from play dough?* Notice if the children are able to use a variety of techniques to explore the materials. Make a note of the children that need further practice in manipulating small objects and plan extra work with malleable materials to develop the appropriate muscles.

Top tip

Remember that children learn best by doing – give them opportunities to handle and manipulate the dough and focus on the process rather than the result, praising all attempts to handle the tools and the play dough. Encourage the children to try several ways to create their object. Provide praise and encouragement to motivate them not to give up.

Differentiation

Support children who find it hard to use small objects with control by providing chunky tools with good rubber grips and by building in time to allow them to practise simple techniques such as rolling and squeezing. Provide an extra challenge by asking the children to add finer details to their objects, such as carving windows into buildings.

Further ideas

- Provide some transport shape cutters for the children to use with the play dough.
- Continue the theme in the sand tray, making roads and buildings using sand toys.

The ticket office

CD-ROM resources

 The lost ticket

 Tickets (Chapter 1)

Early learning goals

 Use their imagination in art and design, music, dance, imaginative and role-play and stories.

 Move with control and coordination.

Setting up

With the children's help, create a ticket office in your outdoor area, using a play tent or house. Print off some tickets from the activity sheet 'Tickets' on the CD-ROM or page 13. Add some play money, a till and a ticket collector's uniform. Park the tricycles outside the ticket office.

Getting started

- Listen to the story of 'The lost ticket' (on the CD-ROM) with the children.
- Remind the children of the ticket office you have made together. Do they have any ideas for how it should be played with? Inspire the children to think of places they would like to buy tickets for. Demonstrate how to fill out a ticket template.
- Explain that two children at a time may play in the kiosk and that a further three or four children may buy tickets to use the tricycles (depending on your own group policy).
- Go into role from time to time with the children and develop their play further by introducing characters such as ticket inspectors, traffic police and so on.

Let's talk!

Say, *Tell me about some times when you might need to buy tickets. What other jobs are there to do at a train station or at an airport?* For children requiring more support, say *Tell me about the game you played with the tricycles.* Challenge the children to retell the story of 'The lost ticket'. Ask, *What information needs to be on a ticket?* Notice how involved the children become in the role-play scenario. Do they develop the story? Note whether the children introduce storylines based on their own experiences.

Top tip

Clearly explain the rules and boundaries for using the tricycles in the outdoor area. Being consistent with rules will contribute to the children's levels of confidence and feelings of security. Recognise that some children may find it difficult to take turns and share the equipment. Model the correct way to ask for a turn and show the children how to play with each other.

Differentiation

Support children by modelling how to ask for a ticket in the ticket office. Play alongside them to introduce some further ideas to enhance their play. Provide an extra challenge by inviting the children to make signs and posters for their ticket office and 'destinations'.

Further ideas

- Listen again to the story of 'The lost ticket' and develop some mimes together for each stage of the story, such as the wind swirling, a magpie flying and so on.

CD-ROM resources

Child's suitcase

Early learning goals

Dress and undress independently and manage their own personal hygiene.

Setting up
Collect a range of dressing-up clothes with different fastenings, suitable for boys and girls, and for 'going on holiday'. Provide some small bags and suitcases.

Getting started
- Show the children the photo of the child's suitcase on the CD-ROM and talk together about what you can see.
- Invite the children to tell the group about times when they have gone away and taken a bag or a suitcase. Encourage them to think about the things that they would need to remember. Write a list on an easel or whiteboard. Explain that you have provided a box of dressing-up clothes for the children to play with. Suggest that they pretend they are going on holiday and tell them that there are bags for them to pack as well.
- In small groups, let the children play freely with the dressing-up clothes and encourage them to manage the clothes independently and also help each other if necessary.
- Praise all the children's attempts at using a range of fastenings.

Let's talk!
Ask the children to help you to decide what you will need to pack to go on a holiday to a hot sunny place. Make a list of their suggestions. Ask, *Why will I need some suncream?* For children requiring more support, ask them to tell you what they have put in their bag as they play – they can take things out and say the names one by one. For an extra challenge, ask *Tell me about a time that you went on holiday – what things did you take?* Notice how individual children join in with the activity. Are they able to use a range of fastenings independently? Do they offer help to other children that need it? Can the children pack a suitable range of clothing for a pretend holiday? Can they explain their choices?

Top tip
Pick up on the children's strengths and warmly praise their efforts – if they have just learned to put on their shoes independently, make sure you 'catch them' doing it! Pass on news to parents about the child's level of independence at the group so that it can be followed through at home (and vice versa).

Differentiation
Support children's development by providing soft toys to dress and undress and toys that require unfastening and so on. Provide an extra challenge by inviting the children to dress up for a specific holiday such as going to the seaside. Ask them to write a list of anything else they will need to pack.

Further ideas
- Have dressing-up races in your outdoor area.

All aboard!

Early learning goals

Build and construct with a wide range of objects, selecting appropriate resources and adapting their work where necessary.

Handle tools, objects, construction and malleable materials safely and with increasing control.

Setting up

Set up an interest table of holiday vehicles, such as boats, ferries, aeroplanes, trains, cars, caravans and so on. Add books showing these vehicles and let the children browse freely. Set up a workshop area with reclaimed materials, card, fixing and cutting materials.

Getting started

- Play the film clip of the plane flying and landing. Watch it two or three times before asking the children to comment. Find out if any of the children have been on holiday in an aeroplane. Ask them to tell the rest of the group about their experiences. Invite other children to tell you about other vehicles they have used when they went on holiday, such as cars or ferries.
- Tell the children that you have provided lots of junk materials and resources in the workshop area for them to use to make a model vehicle of their choice. Ask the children to think about what they might like to make and what they might need before they begin.
- Allow the children to use the materials freely to make a model vehicle, remaining on hand to provide support and to model fixing techniques and how to use the equipment.

Let's talk!

Ask, *What are you planning to make? What things will you need? How does a real aeroplane move? What do you need to include on your aeroplane?* For children requiring more support, ask *Tell me about your model. What things did you use to stick it together?* For children requiring an extra challenge, ask *Tell me how you plan to make the wheels move. Describe how you have fixed your materials together.* Notice if the children are able to select the materials they need. Are they confident at fixing them together?

Top tip

Encourage the children to try several things out before asking for help and suggest that they look at each other's models to give them ideas of how to fix parts together. Pair children with similar interests together and encourage them to talk about their models as they work, consolidating their friendship.

Differentiation

Support children by helping them to select the appropriate materials for the vehicle of their choice. Provide support when fixing materials together, making sure that they try first. Provide an extra challenge by inviting the children to add extra features to their models, such as a space for luggage.

Further ideas

- Make simple model boats from foil trays. Float them and have 'blow-races' in the water tray!

The passport trail

Early learning goal

Write their own names and other things such as labels and captions, and begin to form simple sentences, sometimes using punctuation.

Setting up

Copy the activity sheet 'Passport' for each child (either from page 29 or printed from the CD-ROM). In your outdoor area, place several objects representing places – add a sandcastle to your sandpit; place some boats in your water tray; put some model buildings in an area and so on. Place ink stamps and pads that represent the places you have chosen (such as a boat, a shell and so on) next to the 'places'.

Getting started

- Find out what the children know about passports. Invite individuals to tell the rest of the group about them. Show the children your real passport and how it contains stamps from other countries that you have visited.
- With each child, cut out the 'pages' from the activity sheet and paste the passport cover on to a folded piece of A4 card. Stick the inside page into the passport and stick a further plain piece of paper opposite. Help each child to fill out their details.
- Tell the children that there are some places to visit in your outdoor area. Explain that they will need their passports to visit them.
- Let the children, in small groups, discover the 'places' you have created. Talk about them together and show them how to add the stamp to their passport to show that they have visited it.

Let's talk!

Ask, *What places did you find outside? Tell me about one of your favourite places.* Support children by asking *What did you enjoy about making your passport?* Challenge the children by asking them to tell you about the outdoor trail. *What was good about it? How could it have been better?* Do the children attempt to write words, making use of their phonic knowledge? Are they able to understand the marks they have made? Do they understand that the stamps convey a meaning?

Top tip

Encourage the children to recognise their own unique characteristics as well as those things that they share with others. Using stamps to represent places is a useful tool in developing language skills – using stamps as symbols around your setting can help children to choose and use resources independently.

Differentiation

Support children by scribing their passport details for them, encouraging them to hear some of the initial phonemes as you write the words. Set further challenges such as inviting the children to add extra places to the outdoor area trail. Can they find a stamp to represent that place?

Further ideas

- Use the passports in other role-play scenarios such as a travel agent's or airport.

Passport

Cut out these pages and stick them on to a piece of folded A4 card to make your own passport.

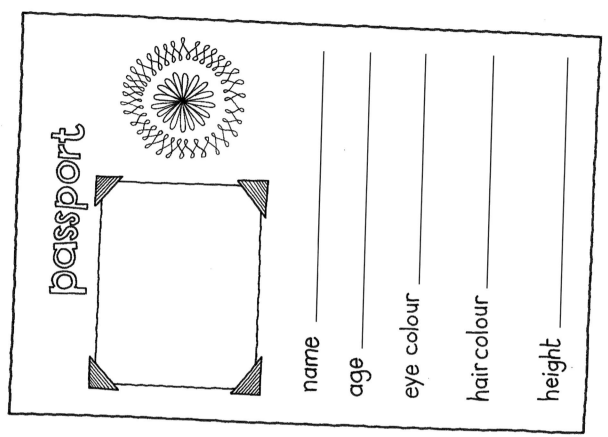

Are we nearly there?

CD-ROM resources

Countryside scene

 Ten vehicles on the road

Early learning goal

Use everyday words to describe position.

Setting up

In your outdoor area or a clear space, set up a large 'car' for the children to pack (made from large building blocks, small chairs, cardboard boxes and so on). Print out a copy of the activity sheet 'Countryside scene', from page 31 or the CD-ROM, for each child.

Getting started

- Listen to the rhyme 'Ten vehicles on the road' on the CD-ROM. Hold up a finger for each line of the rhyme until you get to ten at the end.
- Ask the children to imagine they are going on holiday with their family in a car. Ask them to think about what they will need to pack and what they think the journey will be like. What might they see out of the window?
- Explain that you have made a car for the children to play in. Work with small groups at a time and encourage them to play at packing the car to go on holiday. As you choose things to go in, encourage one-to-one correspondence and counting skills – a case for each person; five blankets; two saucepans and so on.
- When the car is packed, suggest that the children act out the journey, pointing out what they can 'see' along the way.

Let's talk!

Ask, *What do we need to pack? Describe what you can 'see' out of the window. Where is our car going and why?* For children requiring more support, ask *Tell me what you have put in the car.* Challenge the children by asking them *What might you see on a motorway/driving through a town?* Notice whether the children are able to apply one-to-one correspondence to the number of passengers and the number of cases, blankets and so on. Note how many objects they are able to count in an irregular arrangement of objects.

Top tip

Support the children in making choices for what they think should be packed. Be aware of children that speak additional languages and try incorporating their greetings into your game; or use their number system to count objects into the car.

Differentiation

Provide support by asking the children to count out two or three small objects from a group, such as, *We need two saucepans.* Provide extra challenges by asking the children to combine groups of objects, asking *How many cups and plates do we have all together?*

Further ideas

- Give each child a copy of the activity sheet on page 31 and work with them to count the number of each kind of animal or object, writing the numerals in the boxes.

Countryside scene

Count the objects in the picture.

sheep	dogs	houses	farms
	_____	_____	_____
cows	trees	tractors	flowers
	_____	_____	_____

It's a long way

Early learning goals

 Travel around, under, over and through balancing and climbing equipment.

 Use their imagination in art and design, music, dance, imaginative and role-play and stories.

Setting up

Arrange to work in a large, safe and empty space, indoors or outdoors. Set up two or three obstacle courses that require the children to travel in a variety of ways. Provide tunnels to crawl through, obstacles to balance on, objects to climb over and so on.

Getting started

- Talk together about long journeys that the children have made. Look at the photo of the family by the car. Talk about where they might be going and what they might pass on the way.
- Start by asking the children to move around the room like a car going on holiday. Ask them to make the car start and stop at traffic lights, go round roundabouts, climb steep hills and zoom down the other side and so on (be prepared for some engine noise!).
- Next, explain that you have set up an obstacle course for the children to use. Tell them that you would like them to imagine that they are on a really long journey and that they have to go through the obstacles to get there.
- Start the children off and guide them through the obstacles, ensuring that they are developing a range of 'travelling' skills. Invite them to imagine that they are on a journey as they move.

Let's talk!

Say, *Describe how you will move around the obstacle course. Tell me the story of a journey that you have made.* For children requiring more support, ask *How did you travel to the group today? What was the journey like?* Challenge the children by asking, *What sort of obstacles might a car come across on a long journey?* Notice how the children use the equipment. Are they able to use a variety of techniques to travel and move over the equipment? Look for individual ideas and imaginative use of the equipment and space.

Top tip

Make sure that you adapt at least one of the obstacle courses so that all children are able to access it fully. Provide alternatives for children with additional physical needs. Keep in touch with parents to let them know when their children achieve new physical challenges.

Differentiation

If the children find it hard to move imaginatively, then choose other children to demonstrate ways of moving, climbing and travelling. Provide an extra challenge by encouraging the children to complete the obstacle course more than once – each time trying a new way to move.

Further ideas

- Provide small world vehicles and building bricks and other objects and ask the children to make an obstacle course for the cars.

Seaside picture

CD-ROM resources

 A sailor went to sea

 Seaside

Early learning goals

Use their imagination in art and design, music, dance, imaginative and role-play and stories.

Observe, find out about and identify features in the place they live and the natural world.

Setting up

Clear out your large sandpit and rake it over.
Provide a box containing props such as shells, plastic sea
creatures, buckets and spades, pieces of fabric, mini parasols, dolls, cushions and boats.
Set up some small sand trays indoors and provide smaller versions of the same sort of props.

Getting started

- Talk about the photo of the seaside on the CD-ROM. Ask the children what sort of place it shows. Look for as many different aspects of the seaside as possible in the photo and encourage the children to talk about their own experiences and knowledge of the seaside.
- Explain that you have provided a box of objects for use in the outdoor sand pit. Suggest that the children might like to create their own seaside 'picture' with the materials in the sandpit. Ensure that the children understand that damp or wet sand is better to use for sandcastles.
- Tell the children that you also have mini sand trays for use indoors. The children may also create small seaside pictures in these trays.

Let's talk!

Ask, *What would you expect to find at the seaside?* For children requiring more support, ask *Show me the thing you like best about your sand picture. What do you like about it?* Challenge the children by asking, *How could you make your sand picture even better?* Notice how the children engage with their pictures. Do they create a picture that tells a story or do they prefer to make patterns and arrangements in the sand?

Top tip

Understand that some children may still be at the stage where they need to touch and explore the sand. They may prefer to fill and empty the buckets rather than experiment with creating a sand picture. This learning is valid too and must not be rushed if the child is not ready. Observe the children's play so that you are able to identify the right time to intervene with suggestions.

Differentiation

Support children by providing ideas and showing them techniques such as sculpting wet sand.
Challenge the children to use their pictures to tell you a seaside story. Encourage them to play with their pictures, adding interest such as a treasure box and pirate ship and so on.

Further ideas

- Use junk materials to make windbreaks and beach huts. Paint them brightly and add them to the sand trays when they are dry.
- Listen to the song 'A sailor went to sea' from the CD-ROM together.

CD-ROM resources

 Bird feeding young

 In the garden

Early learning goals

 Have a developing awareness of their own needs, views and feelings, and are sensitive to the needs, views and feelings of others.

 Find out about, and identify, some features of living things, objects and events they observe.

Setting up

Arrange for the children to take turns to explore the interactive picture 'In the garden' from the CD-ROM. Set up a large screen for the children to watch the film clip of the bird feeding its babies. Set up an easel or whiteboard ready to write a list on.

Getting started

- Talk together about the interactive picture that the children have been exploring and make a list of all the things that the birds eat. Ask the children to tell you about other things that baby birds might need, such as shelter. Write down the children's ideas.
- Next, look at the film clip showing the bird feeding its young. Talk about the food that it is giving the babies and ask the children to think about the journey the bird might make from its nest to look for food. Where might birds find food in your outdoor area?
- Encourage the children to play outside as mummy or daddy and baby birds. Model swooping and flying around, then going to the 'tweeting' baby to give it some food!

Let's talk!

Ask, *What do baby birds need? What do human babies need?* Support children by asking them to tell you about something they noticed in the interactive picture. For an extra challenge, ask *Tell me what things are the same about baby birds and baby humans? Do they have the same needs?* Notice if the children are able to express their own needs and those that they had as babies. Do they appreciate the needs of other small creatures and are they aware of the similarities between baby humans and baby birds?

Top tip

Reflect on your own practice – are you providing the children with too much help when they need to try some things for themselves? Encourage the children to respect each other's needs – suggest that they try hard to consider other people's feelings when it comes to taking turns and sharing equipment.

Differentiation

Support the children by allowing them to explore the interactive picture again. Work with them and help them to understand the needs of the baby birds. Provide an extra challenge for the children by asking them to draw a picture of a human baby surrounded by all the things it needs.

Further ideas

- Set up a bird table to feed the birds in your outdoor area.
- Share the book *The Baby's Catalogue* by Janet and Allan Ahlberg (Puffin).

The swallow's journey

Early learning goals

Show an understanding of the elements of stories, such as main character, sequence of events and opening, and how information can be found in non-fiction books to answer questions about where, who, why and how.

Observe, find out about and identify features in the place they live and the natural world.

Setting up
Collect some fiction and non-fiction books about the swallow's annual migration, such as *Swallow Journey* by Vivian French (Zero To Ten). Display the photo of the swallows (on the CD-ROM) on a large screen.

Getting started
- Find out if the children have ever seen a swallow or if they know what one is or looks like. Show them the photo from the CD-ROM and tell the children how the swallow spends the summer months in our country, but goes on a long journey to Africa before winter begins.
- Read your chosen story to the children. Share some non-fiction books about animal migrations and demonstrate how to use the index or contents pages to find out specific things.
- Make a clear space and ask the children to 'fly' like swallows with you. Develop three signals for flying, resting and feeding (you could make symbols on cards, or hold up three coloured cards, like traffic lights). Ask the children to fly, rest and feed on your signals.

Let's talk!
Ask, *What is a swallow? Where might you see one? Where do they go when it is winter in our country?* Support children by asking *If you could fly, where would you go to and why?* Challenge the children by asking *What will they need during their journey?* Do the children understand that they can find out about topics of interest by reading and searching through books? Can they make a guess about what is inside the book from looking at the cover and the pictures inside?

Top tip
Make sure that the children get the opportunity to do their own research, rather than simply being fed the information. Judge when a child is ready to be taught new skills such as learning how to search for a topic in books or on websites.

Differentiation
Support children by allowing them to look through the books at their own pace. Encourage them to look for specific pictures of things in the book such as a swallow resting on a wire or a swallow feeding and so on. Set further challenges such as inviting the children to find out about another animal that makes a long journey every year.

Further ideas
- Suggest that the children paint pictures to show the swallow's migration – it could be a farm building, telegraph wire and aerial views of landscapes that the swallows fly over and so on.

From pond to bush

CD-ROM resources

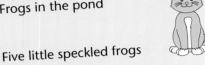

Frogs in the pond

Five little speckled frogs

Early learning goal

In practical activities and discussion, begin to use the vocabulary involved in adding and subtracting.

Setting up

Set up a water tray or paddling pool close to some shrubs or plants in your outdoor area. Provide a basket of plastic frogs.

Getting started

- Listen to the song 'Five little speckled frogs' on the CD-ROM and encourage the children to join in. Teach them how to hold out one arm as the log, with five fingers resting on it to represent the frogs. After each verse, one frog jumps into the pool and there is one less. Talk together about what frogs like to eat and where they live – they don't stay in the water all the time, but make journeys to find insects to eat.
- Show a group of children at a time your paddling pool and frogs. Invite them to play freely with them. Suggest that the frogs sometimes need to go off to the shrubs and bushes to look for food. Use the opportunity to do some practical adding and subtracting.
- Play other games such as totalling the number of frogs in the pool and in the bushes. Continue the fun, playing adding and subtracting games with the frogs – such as *I've got two frogs in the bush and three of their friends have come to join them. How many are in the bush now?*

Let's talk!

Ask, *What do you think frogs like to eat?* For children requiring more support, ask *Give me one more frog – how many am I holding now?* Provide an extra challenge by asking *How many frogs are in the pool? How many are there in the bushes? How many frogs are there altogether?* Notice whether the children are able to apply their mathematical understanding in practical contexts. Do they appreciate that 'more' means that a number will increase and that if some frogs are taken out of the pool the number will be less?

Top tip

Use the opportunity to talk to the children about keeping safe near ponds and water. Never leave them unsupervised around a paddling pool. Give children the time and space to respond when you pose practical problems. You may need to reword questions to suit individual learning styles.

Differentiation

Provide support by working with small numbers and concentrate on addition skills. Provide extra challenges by combining bigger numbers up to ten and switching between addition and subtraction.

Further ideas

- Provide each child with a copy of the activity sheet 'Frogs in the pond' from page 37 or print from the CD-ROM and ask them to cut out their frogs. Practise counting frogs in and out of the pond, varying the task to suit different abilities.

Frogs in the pond

Cut out the frogs. Put some in the pond.

Penguin partners

Early learning goal

Find out about, and identify, some features of living things, objects and events they observe.

Setting up

Research some child-friendly websites to find out information about penguins. Bury some small balls in the sandpit and your outside area. Select a few film clips of penguins making a journey for food to show the children, such as from *Happy Feet* (Warner Bros), *The March of the Penguins* (National Geographic) and *Life in the Freezer* (BBC).

Getting started

- Show the children the photo from the CD-ROM of the penguins and eggs. Talk about it together and find out what the children know about penguins.
- Explain how the daddy penguin keeps the penguin egg warm while the mummy penguin makes a long journey to catch fish to feed the family. Show the children your chosen piece of film.
- Ask the children to find a partner. Explain to them that you have hidden some pretend penguin eggs (balls) in your outside area and sandpit. Ask the children to go and find the egg and then work as a team to look after it – keeping it warm and safe while one of them goes away to fish.
- Encourage them to continue their play as penguin families!

Let's talk!

Ask, *Where can we find information about penguins? What would you like to find out?* For children requiring more support, ask *What did you find out in the film that we watched?* For children requiring an extra challenge, say *Describe how you found out some interesting things about penguins.* Notice if the children are able to use a variety of sources to find out information. Do they understand that information can be found in lots of different forms?

Top tip

Ensure that all the children have equal opportunities to access the ICT equipment during the activity. Allow the children to find out things for themselves but be sensitive to their needs, supporting them as required and extending their ideas with careful questions.

Differentiation

Support children by helping them to interpret the information – after they have watched a film clip, check their understanding and explain it again in simple terms to reinforce the message. Provide an extra challenge by inviting the children to print out information as well as drawing and writing some of their own to compile into a book.

Further ideas

- Set up your water tray with blocks of ice and rocks. Provide toy penguins and sea creatures and allow the children some free play.

Whales and dolphins

CD-ROM resources

Dolphin

Early learning goal

Recognise and explore how sounds can be changed, sing simple songs from memory, recognise repeated sounds and sound patterns and match movements to music.

Setting up

Arrange to use a large clear space for dancing in.
Source some suitable underwater music, preferably including some whale and dolphin sounds, such as *Relax with Ocean Dreams* (Eclipse Music Group).

Getting started

- Show the children the photo of the dolphin from the CD-ROM and play the sound that accompanies it.
- Talk about the long journeys that some whales make each year. Explain that on their journey they are always looking for food. Talk about the hazards and the things that they might pass on their way, such as fishing and other big boats, hunters and sharks.
- Now think about how dolphins move. Dolphins tend to make shorter journeys but they still have to be wary while they travel – protecting themselves and their babies from sharks and fishing nets. They eat while they travel and they have lots of fun jumping, diving, twirling, spinning and swimming fast.
- Ask the children to imagine that they are dolphins on a journey: feeding, avoiding dangers, protecting their babies from sharks and simply enjoying floating and twirling, jumping, leaping and swimming along.
- Play the music you have chosen and invite the children to dance as whales, moving in the way that the music makes them feel.

Let's talk!

Ask, *What food do whales and dolphins eat? What dangers might a whale or dolphin encounter while they are swimming?* For children requiring more support, ask *What does the music sound like? Tell me what the music reminds you of.* Challenge the children by saying, *Describe the music. Tell me the story of your whale or dolphin's journey.* Notice how the children engage with the music. Do they respond to the tempo and the feel of the music by altering the way they move? Are they able to tell a story through their movements?

Top tip

Make sure that the children receive regular sessions where they can move imaginatively in a big space. Encourage them to return to explore dance themes several times to increase confidence and understanding. Model how to watch and praise other children's attempts. Encourage the children to respect each other's ideas.

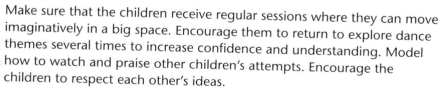

Differentiation

Support children by suggesting two or three ways to move to the music. Stop the music at regular intervals to allow the children to share ideas – this will support those children that need inspiration. Challenge the children further by asking them to think of the story that they would like to tell as they dance. Ask them to tell you their story. For example, *My dolphin has lost its mummy and is looking for food to keep it healthy until he finds her again.*

Further ideas

- Make an 'under the sea' painting or collage (see page 48).

Horse and cart

CD-ROM resources

Working horses

Early learning goals

Use a range of small and large equipment.

Find out about past and present events in their own lives, and in those of their families and other people they know.

Setting up

Make an enlarged copy of the activity sheet 'Working horses' on page 41 and display it. Find some books that show pictures of horse-drawn vehicles. Set up a table with small world horses and construction materials such as Sticklebricks and Duplo. Include some reclaimed materials and further plastic horses. Outside provide large boxes and bamboo canes, pipes and other materials for making giant carts to pull. Set out any trailers that you have for the children to pull.

Getting started

- Share the pictures of the horse-drawn vehicles with the children and talk about them together. Explain that you would like the children to either make their own horse and cart model or play at pretending to be horses, pulling their home-made carts outside.
- Show them the materials that you have provided and ask them to discuss their ideas with you and with their friends.
- Make sure that you and your helpers are on hand to provide assistance when required. Demonstrate techniques for fixing and joining if necessary and offer helpful suggestions to develop the children's ideas.
- Allow the children to play freely, inside and out, with their creations.

Let's talk!

Ask, *What do you think these horses are pulling? What might be inside the carriage/cart?* For children requiring more support, ask *What equipment can you see? Tell me about your ideas for something you could make.* Challenge the children by asking, *What are you planning to make? How will you make it and what will you need?* Notice if the children are confident in using a range of equipment or if they choose things they are familiar with. Make a note of children that explore and experiment with equipment, finding new and imaginative ways to use objects.

Top tip

Give the children sufficient time to play with their creations, and if possible leave the constructions out for further sessions so that the children can develop their experiences and their play. Be aware of children that hang back during the play and try to pair them up with children who will share with them and make them feel included.

Differentiation

Work closely with children requiring support, helping them to make a simple cart shape. Provide an extra challenge by encouraging the children to source their own materials for the construction work.

Further ideas

- Arrange to go on a visit to a museum of country life, a transport museum or a National Trust property that has examples of carriages, carts and caravans or working horses.

Working horses

Talk about the pictures.

CD-ROM resources

Hansel and Gretel

In the woods

Early learning goals

 Select and use activities and resources independently.

Listen with enjoyment, and respond to stories, songs and other music, rhymes and poems and make up their own stories, songs, rhymes and poems.

Setting up

Provide props for the role-play area to create 'Grandma's cottage', such as a patchwork blanket, cushions, a basket, home corner equipment and so on. Select a version of the 'Little Red Riding Hood' story. Set up the 'In the woods' interactive picture.

Getting started

- Read the story of 'Little Red Riding Hood' to the children. Talk about the story together, in particular about the journey through the woods.
- Demonstrate how to use the interactive picture on the CD-ROM and allow the children to take turns to explore it, in pairs.
- Draw the rest of the group's attention to the empty role-play area. Suggest that they might like to set it up as 'Grandma's cottage'. Ask them to think about what they will need. Let groups of up to four children at a time work together to set up the cottage.
- Once the cottage is complete, encourage the children to take turns to play in it – they might choose to use it to re-enact the story, or to act out other traditional tales such as 'Goldilocks' and 'Snow White'.

Let's talk!

Ask, *What things do we need to make Grandma's cottage? Where can we find these things?* Support children by asking them to look at the pictures in the storybook version you have read to them. Ask them, *What things can you see in Grandma's cottage? What things have we put in our cottage?* For an extra challenge, ask *What other traditional stories can you think of that have cottages?* Notice if the children are able to decide on the resources they need to create a cottage. Are they happy to play independently, making choices about what to include and what game to play?

Top tip

Recognise and praise the children's achievements in creating a cottage, asking individuals to show you the part that they contributed and praise them warmly for their hard work. Allocate a key worker to assist a child that wants to join in but needs more confidence to work independently.

Differentiation

Support less independent workers by providing a collection of resources for them to use to set up the area. Provide a challenge by asking the children to look at pictures from the story, making a list of what they need to collect before they start work.

Further ideas

- Share the story 'Hansel and Gretel' found on the CD-ROM. Focus on the journey through the woods and discuss the similarities with other tales set in the woods.

Doing the rounds

CD-ROM resources

Postman

Ten big letters

Early learning goal

Use developing mathematical ideas and methods to solve practical problems.

Setting up

Fill a sack with covered parcels of various shapes, weights and sizes. Locate a copy of *The Jolly Postman* by Janet and Allan Ahlberg (Puffin).

Getting started

- Listen to the rhyme 'Ten big letters' from the CD-ROM and look at the photo of the postman. Invite the children to make a circle and act out the rhyme together, with one child as the post person and the other children being named to collect the post. Show the children how to fold down one finger each time a letter is delivered until you get to zero.
- Next, read the story of *The Jolly Postman* to the children and talk about parcels that the children have received. Still sitting in a circle, present your sack of parcels. Pass the sack around the circle and ask the children to take turns to take one out. Invite them to describe the parcel – encourage them to use shape names and descriptions and any other information that they wish.
- Now work with groups of children at a time to sort the parcels in a variety of ways (by shape, colour, size and so on). Start with the children's ideas and then introduce some of your own.
- Provide other sorting activities around your room and allow the children to select them freely.

Let's talk!

Say, *Tell me about something you received in the post. What shape is this parcel? How else can you describe it? What might be inside this parcel?* For children requiring more support, ask *Tell me what's the same about your collection of parcels.* Provide an extra challenge by asking *How would you sort the Jolly Postman's parcels?* Notice whether the children use describing words or the names of shapes. Are they able to apply sorting criteria consistently?

Top tip

Make sure that everyone who wants to gets a turn to be the post person – either in this session or a subsequent one. Write a newsletter for the children to deliver to their parents with the latest news from your group, including ways to develop the group's topics at home.

Differentiation

Support children by providing the shape words after they have tried to describe an object, saying *Yes, it does have pointy corners. It is a rectangle.* Challenge the children to find other objects to add to the sets they have made.

Further ideas

- Make posting boxes for the children. These can be themed, such as a yellow box for yellow things, or a letter 'a' box for pictures and objects beginning with 'a'.

Off to the shops

CD-ROM resources

Going to nursery

At the shops

Early learning goal

Retell narratives in the correct sequence, drawing on the language patterns of stories.

Setting up

Set up a play shop on a table or in your role-play area. Choose a book about going shopping, such as *Don't Forget the Bacon* by Pat Hutchins (Red Fox) or *Teddybears Go Shopping* by Susanna Gretz (A&C Black). Make a table-top shopping display including shopping books and shopping lists, receipts, food advertisements and catalogues. Make an enlarged copy of the activity sheet on page 45 'Going to nursery'.

Getting started

- Show the children the photo from the CD-ROM of the family shopping and point out the shopping list in the woman's hand. Encourage the children to talk about their own experiences of going shopping.
- Tell the children your chosen story. Invite individuals to remember what happened in the story in the order it happened. On an easel or whiteboard, write down the main points of the story in order.
- Now give the children some choices of play activities linked to shops: playing shops in your set up area; exploring the material on the table top display; play-writing shopping lists and looking at shopping books.

Let's talk!

Say, *Tell me about this photo. Tell me about your own experiences of going shopping. What happens in the story? How does the story begin? What happens in the middle of the story? How does the story end?* Support children by asking, *Tell me something about the story.* Challenge the children by asking, *Tell me about the story, from beginning to end. What other stories do you know about shopping?* Do the children understand the terms 'beginning' and 'end' with reference to a story? Are they able to retell the main points of a simple story?

Top tip

Make sure your play shop contains a variety of foods from different cultures. Support the children's learning in the play shop by adding new challenges as they become ready. For example, provide extra resources for play writing such as pads, sticky labels and card for making signs.

Differentiation

Support children by opening the book at the beginning and asking them to comment on the picture. Reinforce that this happened at the start of the story; repeat the process with a picture from the middle and end of the book. Challenge the children to draw three pictures to represent the beginning, middle and end of the story. Suggest that they caption the pictures to tell the story.

Further ideas

- Use an enlarged copy of the activity sheet, 'Going to nursery'. Cut out the pictures and work with a group of children to tell the story by putting the pictures in the correct order to tell a tale.

Going to nursery

Talk about the pictures. Cut them out and put them in order.

Gruffalo maps

CD-ROM resources

In the woods

Early learning goals

Observe, find out about and identify features in the place they live and the natural world.

Explore colour, texture, shape, form and space in two or three dimensions.

Setting up
Set up an interest table with objects found in the woods, such as twigs, logs, pine cones, small rocks, primroses and bluebells (bought) and so on. Have a copy of *The Gruffalo* by Julia Donaldson (Macmillan) to hand. Set out a table with boards, play dough tools and play dough in various colours and another table with paper and colouring materials. Add small world trees, twigs, plastic plants, pieces of fern, stones and woodland creatures to your sand tray.

Getting started
- Allow the children to explore your interest table. Read *The Gruffalo*, drawing attention to the scenery that the mouse and the Gruffalo pass through. Explain that you would like the children to make a woodland picture based on the story.
- Tell them that they can do this in a variety of ways – they can choose to make trees, logs, plants and paths using play dough and boards; they may play with the resources in the sand tray, creating a sand path and arranging small world toys and natural objects along the way. Or, they may choose to draw their own Gruffalo woods.
- Allow the children to explore the choices freely, making several different versions if they wish.

Let's talk!
Ask, *What creatures can you see in the woods?* For children requiring more support, ask *Which animals does the mouse meet?* For children requiring an extra challenge, ask *Tell me about the animals that the mouse meets – where do they live and what do you think they usually eat?* Notice if the children recognise the features of a woodland from the illustrations. Are they aware of creatures that they might find in the woods? Are they curious to explore the resources on the display table?

Top tip
Together, talk about staying safe on walks, for example, remind the children not to pick wild berries or mushrooms. Ensure that all the children get an equal chance to use the equipment they want for their pictures. Encourage the children to share the resources fairly and treat their friends' models and pictures with respect.

Differentiation
Support children by helping them to develop ways of rolling and manipulating the play dough to make log, tree and rock shapes. Provide an extra challenge by inviting the children to draw simple maps showing the woodland journey that the mouse makes. Provide long sheets of paper and drawing materials, or suggest that they chalk the journey on to the outside surface, adding found equipment to represent rocks, logs and trees.

Further idea
- Let the children explore the interactive picture 'In the woods' on the CD-ROM.

Under, over and through

Early learning goals

Travel around, under, over and through balancing and climbing equipment.

Work as part of a group or class, taking turns and sharing fairly, understanding that there needs to be agreed values and codes of behaviour for groups of people, including adults and children, to work together harmoniously.

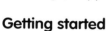
Setting up

Arrange to work in a large clear space and provide a selection of benches, boxes, climbing equipment and hoops, skipping ropes and so on.

Getting started

- Listen to the rhyme 'We're going hunting' from the CD-ROM. Play it again, several times, encouraging the children to join in with any phrases that they remember. As you listen, make some hand actions and facial expressions to go with the words and encourage the children to join in too.
- Now explain to the children that they are going to have a chance to make up their own hunting story, using the equipment you have put out. Together, decide how to use the equipment safely and let the children try it out. Stop at regular intervals to ask the children to describe their movements: *I am going under the climbing frame …*
- Ask the children to imagine that they are going hunting as they quietly and carefully move around all the equipment.

Let's talk!

Ask, *What rules should we have for using this equipment? Tell me all the ways you have found for using the equipment.* For children requiring more support, say *Tell me about something new you have tried today.* Challenge the children by asking *What are you planning to make? How will you make it and what will you need?* Notice if the children are confident in using the equipment in a variety of ways. Do they demonstrate control in their movements? Note if they are able to put together a series of movements into a simple sequence.

Top tip

Make sure that the equipment you provide may be accessed by all children. For example, a child that finds balancing difficult should be given the opportunity to slide along the equipment on his or her tummy. Encourage the children to work with a partner to investigate ways of using the equipment.

Differentiation

Work closely with children requiring support, helping them to try out new ways of moving and using the equipment. Provide an extra challenge by encouraging the children to listen to the rhyme again and make up a series of moves on the equipment to act out the rhyme.

Further ideas

- Share and enjoy the story *We're Going on a Bear Hunt* by Michael Rosen (Walker Books).

Under the sea

CD-ROM resources

Under the sea

Early learning goal

Express and communicate their ideas, thoughts and feelings by using a widening range of materials, suitable tools, imaginative and role-play, movement, designing and making, and a variety of songs and musical instruments.

Setting up

Collect a range of resources about coral reefs including guides to coral reef fish, posters, plastic underwater creatures and the DVD and book *Finding Nemo* (Disney Pixar). Fill a treasure box with ribbons, pieces of Cellophane, scraps of tissue paper, shiny paper, sequins and so on. Set up some tables with paints, paper, scissors, glue sticks and colouring and drawing materials.

Getting started

- Set the scene for an underwater journey. As the children arrive at the group, play the film clip of the coral reef fish from the CD-ROM. Display books, posters and sea creatures for the children to explore.
- Read a version of *Finding Nemo* to the children, or watch a clip from the DVD showing Marlin the clownfish's long journey to find his son Nemo. Talk about all the sea creatures from the story. Look at the pictures in the book and film, as well as the other resources you have collected.
- Tell the children that you would like them to create their own underwater picture. Explain that you have provided a treasure box of materials that they can use to stick on their pictures, but that they may also choose to paint, draw or do a mixture of all the things.

Let's talk!

Ask, *What creatures live on a coral reef?* For children requiring more support, ask *What creatures will you put in your picture?* Challenge the children by saying, *Describe the coral reef you have made. Tell me about your creatures.* Notice how the children engage with the materials. Do they experiment with texture and colour? How do they represent movement in their pictures? Note whether the children are able to develop their own ideas or if they rely on copying other people.

Top tip

Consider individual learning styles – if a child does not have the manipulative skills required for fine collage work, let them create their design using large chalks on your outdoor surface. Encourage the children to try several ways to achieve their underwater effects. Model how to show pleasure in another child's work.

Differentiation

Support children by providing some fish templates for them to draw round. Hold the templates in place as the children draw round them. Challenge the children further by asking them to include three or four different species of underwater creatures in their pictures.

Further ideas

- Transform your role-play area into a mermaid's cave.
- Do a ribbon dance to some 'Under the sea' music, pretending to be fish or jellyfish, dolphins or turtles!